HINGE

HINGE

emily wolahan

The National Poetry Review Press
Aptos, California

The National Poetry Review Press
(an imprint of DHP)
Post Office Box 2080, Aptos, California 95001-2080

Printed in the United States of America
Published in 2014 by The National Poetry Review Press

ISBN 978-1-935716-36-5

CONTENTS

for Nick

How far is it?
How far is it now?

—Sylvia Plath

I'm frightened.
—Sylvie Reavill

Walking off season, the narrow beach, empty

salt-faded houses. Even in this calm water,

a woman could walk in with heavy skirts,

        even in this century,

and keep going, go under, gulp water, confuse

her body until the body reacts,

tries to save itself quite apart

from her mind.
        She knows

she's losing, tires, sinks, and I have no

real faculty to be able to imagine

        lungs filling with water.

The houses scattered afford the sight,

still and gray. A small light affixed

to the furthest tip of the breakwater guides

sailboats, the holiday kind named after wives

and fairytales, to bay.

From the nursery this morning,

you screamed the house down,

your desperate undirected frowns, a fist,

the floor, the foundation for more frustration.

Walking into the water off a New England

shore might be product of frustration

unvoiced, not for lack of trying. Some things

are not suited for language. In the bookstore,

you scream you want a particular fairy book,

each fairy named, its powers afforded

by the seasonal structures of miniature worlds,

for your mother never lets you choose anything,

nothing at all, not once. Only, she knows

what you want. No one can give it to you.

Raindrops hit moving water.

The land of Shelter Island surely lies

at the horizon, not far. Here to there

is one journey I've never tried

to sate a great desire for help, for something,

for satisfaction—which is not really what I want,

but I'm at a loss for quite how

to put it, like when you sometimes ask me

what a word is

        and I try to tell,

but you can barely read a greeting card,

sounding out single letters, not always well,

that o makes an ah sound, not an o sound,

how will you understand?

SLY AND UNSEEN

The infant cannot stop laughing.

In the white gallery, his mother inspects

where concrete meets a burst of dirt feeding

blades. Freshly painted walls abut

                  the grass line guttering.

She watches it fed synthetic sun.

Exhibit: new air, new cycle.

                  The infant laughing.

Below a flat gallery of clouds, the city pigeon

must rise, beating against the volume

of empty space, its intricate layer,

                  feather moving air.

Hollow bones espouse its inaccessible landscape,

push higher, higher, until pressure changes,

oxygen changes and turn then to

plummet in an open marriage to the core.

The backward pump of a bird landing

in the full sway of pregnant trees,

their acknowledgement of captive air.

      To step barefoot on the grass,

to change limbs' mobility, lightness in bones,

coolness between toes and tickled ankle.

            The infant, laughing,

bids goodbye to the room. The room collapses.

It seems phenomenal an animal

can hold still in that air.
         That some solutions

become answers, their spatial disclosure

a forklift of readiness. And the rest:

                our unseen day

carried on and up and away.

ENGLISH CHANNEL, FÉCAMP 1989
after Hiroshi Sugimoto

Gris. Sel. Atlantique.
The expressive lip, a solemn order.

An expanse to view
        inward,
our exaggerated value of needs.

        Gris, a sky.
And more—a patch, a climb
into a stratosphere. Single
transporting article,
        in its resistance, its decision
        to be any of them. One grain in.

Sel. Sand, damp, each step
a stamp and smack,
the fog wanted inland
to cover, to *Atlantique*—

solutions
in reorder. A cold day,
        a camera, a coast.
All variation
within set spectrum.

Horizontal here, elsewhere curved.
And also, a feminine thing
internecine.
        Voici, une mer.

ARGUMENT IN EXUSCITATIO

The house in the distance but not so far
it can't be seen between two tall pines,

down a gravel drive, the checkered roof
a minor indication. I stayed there briefly.

Coming out of a blood haze and into waking
inside a full-length mirror, a border not

easily maneuvered, shirked off, defiled,
told to go to hell.
                    One could miss

the dark wood siding, several high hedges
overgrown and vined, the place abnegated

since they put in land mines, tore up the road.

When I write they, it is of course another

pronoun I mean, and I, of course, a vast
misunderstanding of desire.

                    Behind the house are wildflowers,

a view of the valley, a bench to take it in,
and the clouded breaking into finery. I write

"birdsong," "pinecone," "dulcet evening shore"—

continuing cobbles together a Roman solution
now invisible, overrun by the locals long dead.

I can see the window glass is broken,
near white wisps erect in the sky. I write

"There is something I've wanted to say"
            and "You have no idea."

A blanket of needles out of the sun. Dank green

moss on my shoes, depressions that trigger
an explosion of latent, baneberry, lavender.

HER TINY UNIVERSE BECOMES IMMENSE

One cries at this.

Another sleeps through it.

We now have a future of arched
        bridges and cathedral spires.

Now we have each other—

There is no sleep that cannot be interrupted—
her small ear not an inch
from such a small brow.

EMBLETON BAY

This incredible wager of better

sets off the campaign; its brightness burns

out the edges, splits itself as long tracks

of seawater finger the beach, then unite.

The vacation homes on the bluff

spread their empty approach over rain,

severing clouds.

Often the size of things

confuses me. Some appear hideous,

engorged like painted balloons,

their faces stretched so far the colors

pale. We find ourselves standing

on dank sand, sinking and silent. How old

it all looks. The light somehow abandoned

post-apocalypse. The architectural features

bred between wars.

I will climb inside

the bristles of that bare bright hedge

and winter until a swimming-pool-blue

horizon.
Then I'll unpack.

Some kelp has clumped on the sand,

the moat around it deepening as the sea

retreats. Tendrils fanned, its glisten

bodily and internal. We can try.

And the payoff increases and the loss.

We follow a path into the dune grass—

Oh, motley solutions, tools, promises:

you are holding back the sea.

QUITE COLD IN CLOUD

Laying down, she lows
        heft and black,
under the vast, open and black.

Elemental obscured,
        a figure deep in the dark cave,
speaking clearly.

        Darkly
        she moves.

The insistent exit can be found
in night field, short wheat
        bundled in shadow.

The sharp odor of earth working a kinned low
energy, swallowed birth. What is that
        cresting the stand of trees—

Who cannot return?

TERRA INCOGNITA

Manner of bend, the new night time,

earlier now, cooler, moon pounding.

We stand looking at the wide sky over a harbor

as ships tack and bend the several parts

of civilization into public, the space to which

we refer, small victories of agreement, a civil

reddening. I commit to the indiscriminate,

increasingly Gospel, leaning on the barrier,

nearly diving into the harbor

which won't be sea for several miles.

Red evidence of curve, stretching out

as kids swing fishing rods, cast and attend

to other rods, laughing, impressing the girls,

who are laughing. A tenable now, immersed

in churned waterways, calling to its transient

population. What exactly do we plan to do?

For each reel, there is line, float,

disruption of surface, line, bait, hook.

One silent departure for each taut agreement.

In everything we're not saying, a lucent rise.

HARD SOFT BODIES
after Kiki Smith

To face it best no face.

Universe the universe
imagined red and luminous.

It needs to turn.

A line corded in braid ever of flesh,
rinse and tether,
          ever curved,

both rest and kick
rest and not;

built from inside
to outside covered

and then individual.

It needs a face.

Its sides
spatulaed.

          The face
first exits misshapen
          misplaced.

WIDE: LETTER TO HERSELF

Your dystopian landscape—
sheep gutting grass, ocean tearing at land,

spitting it back.

Exterior drowned
in a mixture of sod,
sodden, sexless.

> Sifted, slated to routine,
> a sunless morning, banked fire,
> the diadem of hedge dew.

Oh, no—thank you.

> You are convenient, I can afford you—
> but no thank you all the same.

*** *** ***

Go back to the bridge

right to the center

and from there send me a text of three words

I miss you

                                    *** *** ***

My kitchen will do as receptacle.
Several, small.

Within kitchen, drawer,
within drawer, this porcelain bowl.

It will do. Will do.

*** *** ***

Pose of transformation
taken, for the time, as paradise.

Sleepless, slightly ill,
deficient in beauty.
Reminded of the

indecision of paradise.

You clomp in from the field,
a spatter of mud across your
left cheek and wear it
for the morning.

*** *** ***

And hatred comes slowly,
the room tinged blue.

What have you got to lose
to turn away?

Quickly.

You must turn away.

*** *** ***

Encased behind glass:
        a dozen glasses.
Each removed, eventually washed,
returned. Say what you want

a certain way—
maybe you'll get it.

                                          *** *** ***

Swivelled angle, words shattered,

the woman's face
        now confident,
        now frail.

So frail you can barely hear it.

Light rain, cotton rain, cashmere rain.

Her dangerous belief in expertise.

Instant of radical

Instant of review—

    Language muffled to a symphonic hush

Instant terrorizes and dangles

        What is fiery

        Draws in

        Arms attached to shoulders

        Organs tucked neatly ready to slip

        At any opening

Instant rends

Instant cleaves

        Soft music and soft shoe

        The long respite

        A middle room

I AM TETHERED
TO THE POINT OF DISCOVERY

The hoar frost spikes
and shivers.

Our riverbank path is wet.

We've all forgotten.

Wolves have retreated into
their huntsman wood, some cry
bells out, its ringing
matched by a greeting of delicate
hollow things and the glacial
groan deeply rooted.

Rapid movement under thin
river ice.

How the frozen
tree breaks
branches, pulling
its own weight.

_____

The white matter of sky unhinges to spit

a scatter, the sort that accumulates quickly,

drenches. You out there in your clothes.

Me in here in my clothes. Left to ask

and ask, what precisely is

our arrangement? Green branches spindle

over a hedge's suggested height, the material

of newly paved roads bends in the distance.

Each one creaks open, their cranked yen

       unsatisfied. The earth drinks it up.

Birds shelter to encompass and produce

our grand scheme in real-time concentration.

Winging out space beyond the moderate peaks

of houses I stare past,

beyond the mouth of the river, beyond

stagnant, static color, middle lost

to dull light, they softly cluster

under our high cover
                in this narrow passage fully dry.

SUNRISE (MIRROR, GRAY)

after Gerhard Richter

Clouds goose down—fast moving, northeast.

Shipping news for Hendon, Whitburn,

Seaton Sluice, Blyth. That shaggy pine

chuckles. The neighbor's custard

yellow window lit. My kettle on.

The great night weight,

pressed, lifted, comes down again.

To awake to this.

Overhead, seagulls sweep north.

The roof creaks, pushing its claims

and inside, deep inside, a self in throes.

Elbow to hip, knee to chest, hand to face.

To face. To face.

Red cheek—

Oh, look at you, gray morning.

Your certain, reflective quality.

The surface changes and moves east,

out to the North Sea, on to Holland, and

losing, it's let loose.

                    I'm awake.

That little topiary in my neighbor's yard

kowtows to an imaginary king. A wood pigeon

struggles to land. The gulls hover,

dive. Balancing without flapping wings:

little control, also, little energy.

She's on the edge out here.

Mountains, valleys, mountains.
Plains, hill, beach, ocean.

She's on the edge out here and it occurs to her:
                        can she take this
                        as a test?

Stephanie starts the car,
starts a new entry into space.

Look at this as we move forward: Wind
blowing palms like they're under water.

            A short couple jogging to make
            the short light.

            Sunlight altering its position as we turn.

            Sunlight altering its position
            as we turn.

Stephanie sits at the foot of the bed
yawning, slow to start the next day

in an outpost where only surface
resonates.

This signifies a certain that.
The palms spread and retract.

Her hands on the wheel, neck craned,
line of sharp burn
altering its position as we turn.

SILVER LAKE MORNING

An alternating beauty—

my front door ajar,

an orange petal, a sudden sharp

stream of rising light, the tchuck and

spray of the neighbor's sprinkler.

I remain at my door.

A single person in space

          accounts for the other things

in that space: Walls, frames on

the walls, her own room as she awakens.

This is all she can see and thinks,

         we call that *taupe*,

that one *mauve*. The morning rises,

synchronized sprinklers burst forth.

A perfectly aligned concrete path

has been poured from my doorstep to the street.

The cement nearly white.

A child pressed in her palm, used a stick

to write her name.

This is *quantifiable*.

This is *concrete:*

my palm flat, hand raised

as though to signal stop.

WHEN WE WEARY, WHAT ART?

Not love of flesh
nor fabric, nor chocolate.
Not quest. Not mechanic.
Not prick of finger.

Not transformation.
          Despair becomes container—
of the Wind or Mind—
shifts caution beyond design

to interiors. The architecture
          of those interiors.

Not hair nor skin nor candlelight.
Dispensary depot of sky,
the view from a window, roof tops.
          A runner passing
and then another
and then another.

The first returns. Not chair.
Not desk. Not lamp.
               An arched door pushed open
               by a bicycle back wheel.

The cross section of sky and shaftway
               constitutes a fruitful day,
a meeting on the street. Knowledge of
the smaller parts of industry. Of wire
          of yellow, of trombone.

EXUANT

A rehearsal

as far as you can see. Diminishing rows

of chimneys, telephone poles,

naked arms reaching

past the frost to the sky utterly clear.

Steam rises from a distant boiler.

Unfinished jigsaw,

pine silhouette. The frost removes all shadows;

roofs are cleaned to angled

planes, light's second lattice

over garden—over grove—over garden.

An overgrown soft wood yet to flower yellow.

THE HARBOR ARTS

Stop.
There is a purified border
to your body:
                    interiority, the record
of every discussion.
                    Return to your desk
to find work, like sleep, a full occupation
in physical stillness.
            More comfortable,
                    more lucky.

In an elephant's glorious howdah,
            you are transported
beyond by the second, by a mountain
pass. What bisects? Which touches limits?
Eyes closed,
            each subtle movement mapped
loops back to the question:

            Hold on.
                    Hold up one minute.

*** *** ***

Can we return to this place?

To desire, to quench desire,
to future affairs of the world
        taking place under our noses.

                    They rise up, newly new.

The dunes of Dhaharan shift one centimetre.
Can we return, even against
decree? Against future extremities
we cannot ignore?
                    The eye shifting
open, closed, live feed sating,
            climbing inside to view:
vista, valley, cragged cliff,
too much. Body was one.
            Body was empty.
Its very convenient use of opacity.

                            *** *** ***

In this preserved, empty land,
what can you return with?
        Each part melted,
mixed into an alloy, fused
to maker and scene.
                There's a dog
barking down the beach, in moonlight,
which the artist captured precisely—
cresting the waves just so, wedding
pale blue and white.

                In this, your singular eye
        may be pulled apart.

Oh, to be known. Oh, to know.

When I look at you I desire
        to be known.

        And, in this,
        reunified.

                                *** *** ***

North or off east?
We cannot read the it of it.

Headed out to sea, our ship
      cuts water.

Tight coldness, limb exhaustion,
field of stillness
where the moon
        makes water rise

into a corner of ocean, Gulf of Maine.
We came out here to glimpse

the infinite weight.
        Expanse we cannot push
fast enough or at all well.

          To come to it as
different. To watch it differ. There, below

the surface, five white marks against thick
black skin. It breaches, dives—the water is not

dissimilar to the sky.
        We scan our horizon for dark
marks, floating logs, or exactly.

        *** *** ***

Can you return to this place?
To have known, must know. To know
in the future.
                    Double back to the shape
of the object which entered your grasp.

You will outlive it.

Centuries ago, they couldn't conceive
of millions filling out tax returns,
online questionnaires, checking in
for a transatlantic flight to choose a
                              window seat.

Your stint as a sailor will grow into love
unsparing and silent, the equal of the sun
inside your room,
          an expensive thing.

     Can you? Can I? To this place?

                              *** *** ***

Private industry has come home.
        Me filling the space
        you have created.

I've started and voyaged, vowed and tripped,
worked silently at a desk facing a wall
in an otherwise empty room.

        My humble outfit to input the innermost.

How calm your face, how exterior
I find its concentration.

        Soften. I release
the most boring details of your life,

        tightly wound and winding.

ARGUMENT IN OPTATIVE

The mood, the place, the illuminated building

golden and empty, its construction stalled,

all movement in this area is stalled

as in another. So enter lack, sky whitening

in a winter sunset, its hollowed-out stories,

structural posts keeping the building's long,

flat concrete floors from slapping one

onto the other. Recall the marigold

that breaks into a thousand pieces

leaving us to pine for its solid gathering.

The train ascends the bridge, climbing out of

dense, vivid brickwork into span.

There is blue mixed in the white, a diluted

but careful sense of girders uniting a canyon

dispersed over river water. The momentary

winging out of city and passage, a near return

to complete non-sky, unsure of how far away,

how near. Netting encloses the site,

loosened and caught in the wind, flapping open

to reveal a pale façade.

It's not that I'm unsure. It's something else.

You never said northern air was a cure-all
for demented spirit, but I plunged in crying,

Cure me. Sunset, castle, tidal bank:
I am weary. I shouldn't have thought finding

color in a bleak landscape or bloom
briefly achieved meant much.

You and I consist of the line between
this place and that, a nose forever

for bounty, a craving for boon.
We find carved from the moorland

one farm field abutting an oak grove
sheltering the farmhouse convenient

to its barn, dull pebbledash, a slightly tawdry
hedge, the washing line, a broken-down car

and the corrugated barn roof nearly detached,
its inconsolable drip grooving the concrete.

The red flowered window boxes garish, too
red to be real, a warning flag to all who frame

the hill with windshield and rearview mirror.
For it will not be saviour nor salve.

Despite the track that leads to the house,
a child's finger-painted sea taped

to an upstairs window, the flowers,
nor the washing line will do anything

but stare as we hold each other very far
from the home that home now seems.

       Our mission to the hinterlands.
We'd hoped to retrieve some bell heather,

an asphodel, but nothing here wants us,
knows what to say, nor begins by asking.

ÉCOLE DES HAUTES ÉTUDES

Fine strokes of ink in the margins

along the rooflines, into the ginnels,

a budget for every day of the new year.

The industrious hurry off to work,

a bus swishes by. Try asking the teenager,

legs stretched long, bisecting the front door

of his parents' Chinese takeout,

what it's like to wait for something to happen.

She had promised to change

everything and meant it, promised investment

and said, *As I eat this money, a life will grow.*

I will inhabit and populate it.

And what cannot be studied?

Her syntax encapsulates the blue light

pulsating from a street corner.

How signage soothes. The social science

in each step forward. Buses fill up,

release. The teenager rises to stand

at the door of Double Happiness;

its neon light switches off. What is taught

at the *école des hautes études*, where she's

ensconced, cultivating the connections—

her money languishing in a roux?

She thinks, *High thoughts*.

Great bridges.

Her bus arrives, blue lights shine on,

that friendly operation.

Winter sky the color

of an ocean's desert where great whites

cruise for mates,

their haggard mouths open.

It has been so long

since the sky felt full of itself,

full of another.

Been a long time out there

in the deep.

Three kinds of birds flurry,

scatter after the same morning feed.

Looking up

I prospect the sky for—what?

Beyond the blue, its stratosphere

is unlit and empty—

        unless I continue rocketing

out to space where I'm sure to hit

a meteor, Saturn, Pluto.

They dangle in some third-grade classroom

where the lights are dimmed

and kids watch a shark

        swim eerily smooth

across a TV screen.

It makes so few movements,

is so often alone, driven

by its stomach and, finally,

its need to propagate.

The clear, blue sea—

        empty. The sky

cleared of birds. A great expanse

within me resonates and

I am in space.

                Seagull. Crow. Finch.

The sun crests,

low clouds rise. Dense snow

clings to eaves.

                I begin steady,

(Horizon and above.)

                struggle to keep up.

(Horizon. Above.)

EVERYTHING WITHIN

Laid out before us and receding fast,
a field light lined,
overturned, hay-bundled
                    —ordered and distant.

Conquered land, stupid sheep,
a complex of mills producing.

That distant, dissipating wisp of smoke.
The dank purple of broken-up soil.

Happily stupid. Each to the other
          what the other loves.

Each destroying the other's appetite.

VACANT

Better not.

       Embrace the countryside,
pierce the interior,

circle what crimes of a century can be
discussed and dissected

           to an audience
of two. The brain bred something

fathoms apart from our land,
our population.
               Better find

a hollow tree and, upside down,
compose a staircase of gratitude.

What I meant when I said
I'll stay here forever.

NAKED WOMAN, HER REPOSE

A quiet, doleful state between two
stages of sleep. Pooling skin

purple and yellow, mottled.
And okay (really) with her elephantine

dominion on the settee in the middle
of the room. Tell her what is troubling you.

Please, go on. We are harvest, she says.
People, as animals, interest me.

The mirror image of her face reads
portrait, inhales its comfort with parameters.

Even in January, we remember summer heat,
slow movements. Skin. Deep breaths.

Curled beside the dog-animal, a snout
resting in hand, ribs shuddering, a whiff

of newly installed carpet warmed
by afternoon sun. Not "no clothes"—

rather the expanse of eyes on her and through.
She continues with what she's saying.

The light on her hair emanating misdirection
in the mirror. She says, *We have space our own.*

She says this so that you might gaze, shifting
your weight back and forth, tilting your head,

and think, *Those aren't really her eyes—*
that's just paint. How is it then I know
                                    what she is thinking?

PAUVRES PETITS EN ÉTÉ

Those clement months, we combed
cattails, cicadas crashed
through new houses erasing yellow
from the sky. The high school hall buzzer

still rang every morning. All beginnings.
All what leads to inner tubing the cold,
empty river, sun-burnt boys splashing,
girls half-shitting sun. It's not afternoon

freezing up, not yesterday asleep, the sky
one-third lead. Best be full of bodies.
The one color of now maps its fortress,
the crepuscule, the elm under which cattails

line shallow creeks, refining flat stones.
On those we existed, pummelled, caressed,
cold. On those we waited a long time
so that we became full of seasonal

bodies. Another fall-summer, spring-winter.
Where it seems most impossible, it happens—
white gives way to green, blooms to red,
unsure of coming. Better these bodies crash

empty and inner. Better we comb our cattails,
eat the heads. Eat away at bodies
and produce; don't forget the babies.
Yes, we can still wait. Look—

who are they peering in? Long and rippling
against this range-rimmed sky. Does our water
look different from the other side? They don't
seem to be looking at us—

            do they see only themselves?

PERPETUAL NOON

Atlas spreading out to islands,
their recycled borders.

                      Blue and white

and fantasy.

Light edging through a blind
one thousand miles away.

Illumined, observed
           there and gone.

We own all this real estate in
one embrace.
           Lured forward
by a bladed field, silver and
racked in wind.

           There is that simple job we yearn for.
Going over the interview
           endlessly in our minds.

VINCENT À THÉO
after the Van Gogh correspondence

Via this point
one finds a place.

This point via which
future is past. Line via
points extended
and this is. A garden.

From my back door
I see plot.
Walls. Swallows
collecting grass seeds.

I transfer it to paper via hand.

Find my peace in earth, crop, cycle.
Peace via. This.
Garden. Ringed
in oriental bamboo.

*** *** ***

Saturated in self-teaching.

The skirt is made to slowly rise up the thigh.
Stroke out a breast.

Supplicate your minor ennui
that comes on in afternoon
and be satisfied.

By your own self.

Paint in thick flat strokes
of stylized import.

Soon Théo. The solution's just there.

*** *** ***

Within an elected frame.
Emotive look.

With *Campagne sous la neige*.

In its heavy fall—
pre-melting morning.

A weighted chill within determines
my emotion one over two—attention
becomes a prioritizing of detail.

This removal world
where hands in filtered sunlight
reach across the table. Into space.

*** *** ***

Next is what follows.
Included here a small sketch. A branch

almost in flower.
The tiny part
of the almond tree.

Just here, dark bark,
naked to the nightstand.
It's held in a wine bottle
I emptied last month.

Here is evidence I've been working.

In your next reply
you might request
these blooms in oil.

*** *** ***

Behind the scent—

that is impossible to relay.
Dusk.

Birds feed and crowd the small square.
You sip your wine
and prepare dinner. Sliced courgette.

There is a satellite I've created
to stand away from you.
Around you. And eclipse—
Théo, I see

your son hand you
his favorite train car.
You place it on the playing record.
Close to center. Quick
rotations. These traveled miles.

BEAUTIFUL PARANOIA

Difficult retirement, a gentler chorus.

The skeined transition turns
to light in giddy exhaustion.

Every part of your day will be
                         this part of your day.

                    And yet,

the postman manages to reach
            each number in its turn.
The residents squander another afternoon.

An armor is constructed from romantic movies,
angles of color and the blanket cloud
of something gathering.

ARGUMENT AFTER ECSTASY

Vision and actuality on a track
measured by fallen oak
leaves and ash.

                 Clattered mud
pushed off earth with footstep, boot
      lift,

         depression,
               lift.
The fogged out leaves,
damp and northern. A shag,
       a square—

       I have had my vision.

There is no emperor to offer his thumb
as perfect measure

nor can each progression be
accounted for, every discrepancy
              mapped out for actual.

You go off into the woods and sink
into composting leaves,
          fungi,
               fallen trunks.

You other one, you branch.

Concentrate—

one line, another and now,

now you have had it.

SHEERNESS AS SEEN FROM THE NORE

after J. M. W. Turner

Instead, water laps a low wall.

A dock crane's long yellow arm
dipping slowly,
its afterimage arresting the sun.

We are silent together, those are the rules,
forms articulate in burning light
at the edge of our city, the precipitate
salt marks ringing levels
of deep and shallow.

The man in his boat looks at us squarely,
his pipe, the smoke
on the mountain beyond.

Or perhaps that's a low cloud. His boat
handling higher waves,
a gull in privacy, its mouthful.

In this light the bay looks shallow—
                from here to New Jersey
wading water, flat bottom barges
skirting ruin.

We are filled upon acquaintance
with light as it is acquainted with water
ship, bird, land. Upon meeting you,
a space created and filled,

the problem of how to convey
a distant low cloud
not a problem until decided upon.

Sheerness as entrance to the sea.
The sky peaked and vast and us,
our instruments to navigate color
spread across canvas, the paint dries and hangs,

a barbarism precious,

the greater understanding of two approaches,

like your voice on the phone
and me imagining your face. I imagine
rapid thugs of the helicopter pulling
itself into the sky. The creak of these ships
moving politely past.

For she was the maker of the song she sang,
its distance,   its panel of judges.

For she, the she, even if she didn't
want to. Those tracks curving off, disappearing

were all the while her sentry for return.
             There was a song sung about return,

an unwritten letter with which she was meant
to come to terms.
                    Her evidence
        of the pre-existence of her plan:

the pedestrian bridge newly painted durable
green by the city council. Who can resist

a city that cares? A hum hastens always
toward her, along the musical mantra

        what else   what else.

What is at stake beyond the penetrating
glance, beyond her deep core clenched—

        where the explosion might harden
into a single definition. Might tell her
        this is all you are—

only she,

maker,

knows the little ditty floating forever
further away.
She sings it over and over until

she believes it. The only guarantee is a world
in transition. She once spent Saturdays shut in

watching filmed stage productions of minor
mid-century drama.
She once understood herself
displaying the greatest control of movement,

her heels clacking an echo into the darkness.

Another guarantee:
seduction and transition,

one and the same. Another: there are at least
two more guarantees.

She desired and chose,

traversed the wooden floor without obstruction,
in surprising suburban consonance. As a woman,

she's coming to terms with it. That's her song,
even-colored in plunging and mountainous chords.

When she peered, pirouetted, readied
to change again, what proof

in the hum hee ha of a town
that proudly cares for its pavement,
                    its paths, its bridges.

ACKNOWLEDGEMENTS

Many thanks to the editors of the following journals in which versions of poems from this book first appeared:

Omniverse, Gulf Coast, The National Poetry Review, Boston Review, New Linear Perspectives, DIAGRAM, elimae, and *Mom Egg.*

"L. A. Pale" is for Stephanie Wolahan.
"Vincent à Theo" is for Kevin Wolahan.
"Her Tiny Universe Becomes Immense" is for Sylvie Reavill.

Thank you to C. J. Sage and the National Poetry Review Press for selecting this manuscript and bringing the book into being. Thank you to Ethan Hon, Laura Goode, and Dawn Marie Knopf for their careful reading of these poems at several stages and their always insightful advice. Many thanks to Timothy Donnelly and Mary Jo Bang for fostering a delight in the life of the mind, the pursuit of a perfect line, and leading by example in generosity and support. Thank you to the community of writers I've had the good fortune to join, build up, and be a part of, in particular: Sara Femenella, Dan Bevacqua, Amy Mackelden, Ira Lightman, Joshua Thomson and Marni Ludwig. Much gratitude for the unwavering support of my parents, my sister and my brother.

Thanks to my English family—the Coopers, the Kays, and the Reavills—and my Newcastle friends, who shared their homes and country with me. Thank you to Nick Reavill for his love and belief. Thank you to our children Sylvie and Franklin for their joy, kindness, and inquiry. And thank you to all those who have been near me, or whose words have been dear to me, during the course of writing this book.

Also from The National Poetry Review Press

Lucktown by Bryan Penberthy

Bill's Formal Complaint by Dan Kaplan

Gilgamesh at the Bellagio by Karl Elder

Legend of the Recent Past by James Haug

Urchin to Follow by Dorine Jennette

The Kissing Party by Sarah E. Barber

Deepening Groove by Ravi Shankar

The City from Nome by James Grinwis

Fort Gorgeous by Angela Vogel

Able, Baker, Charlie by John Mann

The Wanted by Michael Tyrell

Loud Dreaming in a Quiet Room by Betsy Wheeler

Guest Host by Elizabeth Hughey

Manual for Extinction by Caroline Manring

Inappropriate Sleepover by Meg Johnson

Porthole View by Lynne Potts

Red House over Yonder by Stacy Kidd

A Lesson in Smallness by Lauren Goodwin Slaughter